Conversations Cover Art

The Lord showed me two pages billowing in the wind, and like sails, they were full of life and expectant. One side showed the past, representing all of God's promises; the other was the new beginnings of the story He was writing for the future, Psalm 91, to trust in His plans and know that I am protected. Cascading down the spine was a blue tassel, a division, a marker of the new season He was leading me to. His rainbow of promises were pouring out from the heavens, engulfing and washing over this prophetic vision. What was coming down from heaven could be seen on the earth. It was causing a tsunami, a turbulent sea. There was a washing away, a cleansing over the pages of the book between the past and the present. There may be a storm on the horizon, but God has you in the boat; He has total control. Trust in the Lord for the promises He has made. There is a new chapter being written.

When you pass through the waters, I will be with you; and when you pass through the rivers, they will not sweep over you.
Isaiah 43:2 (NIV)

First published in 2024
Text and illustrations © Lynne Hudson 2024
All rights reserved. No portion of this book may be reproduced, distributed, or transmitted in any form, including photocopying, recording, or other electronic or mechanical methods in any form without permission from the publisher.

Lynne Hudson
lynne@lynnehudson.com
www.lynnehudson.com

Conversations With the King

Authored & illustrated by
Lynne Hudson

Dear beloved daughter,

I invite you to partner with our Heavenly Father and to embrace His visions and words. Meditate, ask Him what is on His heart for you as you go beyond these pages, and look into the depths of His eyes to behold the thoughts that He has for you. Every "conversation" has a relatable message just for you. He has a loving story to share with you through each page. Sit and enter into His deep presence and let Him have a conversation with you about what He would like to reveal to you. Imagine having a cup of tea with your best friend and sharing your inner thoughts. This is what our Heavenly Father is waiting for—to spend time with you and to partner with you.

These intimate visions and words that I have written are from our Father's loving heart and I know He wants to engage with you and tell you His unique whisperings just for you. Be blessed as you spend time with our Father through these pages. Use this book as your own personal journal. Process the words, visions and scriptures with Him. Go on a journey of revelation with our King.

Beauty For Ashes

Dear Daughter

God uses the darkness that we emerge from and brings beauty from ashes. Step out of the history of darkness where there is no hope. Feel the comfort of being enrobed with Christ's righteousness. Feel this newfound freedom and an awareness of His love as it pours out and blankets the past. Receive the new growth of the future He has for you. Believe that this is a new start. The past is gone, and the new budding life is the glimpse of the future generations that will be birthed into His righteousness because you have taken this first step. The slate is wiped clean. This daughter of the King has her glory sandals on and is ready to walk out the destiny of the plans He has for her.

To appoint unto them that mourn in Zion, to give unto them beauty for ashes, the oil of joy for mourning, the garment of praise for the spirit of heaviness; that they might be called trees of righteousness, the planting of the Lord, that he might be glorified.
Isaiah 61:3 (KJV)

Dear daughter,

God showed me a simple vision of a person's hand reaching out and grabbing a hold of a rope. This person was fearful, lonely and desperate. God was showing this person to depend on Him, and not to focus on the circumstances around them but rather on Him. He is their answer. There was a flower thriving from the vine. We are the flower and Jesus is the vine of new life.

REACH OUT

I felt the Lord saying...
"God is offering a lifeline—the rope. The rope represents God's strength to pull you out of any situation. Grab a hold of His invitation to His peace, freedom, love and mercy. Reach out and connect to His all-encompassing Fatherly love. Step into His arms and receive the blessings and new beginnings."

Let the joy of the Lord fill your void.

Here's what I've learned through it all: Don't give up; don't be impatient; be entwined as one with the Lord. Be brave and courageous, and never lose hope. Yes, keep on waiting—for he will never disappoint you! Psalm 27:14 (TPT)

Dear daughter,

I saw a vision of a delicate flower budding. At the centre of the flower was a rich, singular flame. Small fires were burning at the base, which looked like small budding leaves, but they turned into rich, fiery flames. I saw five leaves supporting, protecting and surrounding the flower. May His grace, favour and fivefold ministry be upon you as you receive your specific callings. May the Lord's strong hand prepare and anoint you for His work. The stem was pliable and able to bend to His ways. The base roots took hold of the rich soil. The journey was fluid and the path was highlighted with His glory.

The fire within.

I felt the Lord saying...
'Keep your centre flame burning for your evangelistic ministry, propelling you into the nations. You have the ground of rich soil where your seeds have been planted. The saints go before you to the nations. Keep the fire burning and radically speak out my love, for you are encased in the breath of the Holy Spirit. The roots are the new wine, spreading into new lands. There is a powerful strength to boldly harvest your crop. I am protecting you. You are cradled in my hand."

...his word is in my heart like a fire, a fire shut up in my bones. I am weary of holding it in; indeed, I cannot.   Jer. 20:9 (NIV)

Dear daughter

The Father blessed me with a loving vision of a little girl crying. She was in despair but cradled in His hand. He always sees our pain and our tears and comforts us with His everlasting love.

Oceans of Tears

I felt the Lord saying…
"We may feel transparent and vulnerable, but God sees our pain, our loss, and our tears that fill the oceans. He always has us in the palm of His hand—showering us with the wrap-around comfort of His fatherly love—a love that can never be matched or extinguished. His love dries our tears and turns our sorrow into joy."

….I HAVE HEARD YOUR PRAYER AND SEEN YOUR TEARS; I WILL HEAL YOU. 2 KINGS 20:5 NIV

"YOU HAVE TURNED FOR ME MY MOURNING INTO DANCING; YOU HAVE LOOSED MY SACKCLOTH AND CLOTHED ME WITH GLADNESS, THAT MY GLORY MAY SING YOUR PRAISE AND NOT BE SILENT. O LORD MY GOD, I WILL GIVE THANKS TO YOU FOREVER! " PSALM 30: 11-12 ESV

Dear daughter,

God gave me a vision of a hummingbird zeroing in on the centre of a sunflower, which looked like a target. The sunflower was full of different shades of brown seeds. The bird was brightly coloured, representing an array of heavenly promises. The feathers looked like flowing sections of material that were free to blow in the wind. It reminded me of worship flags. The orange is for courage and the green is for new life. The sunflower is growing tall and strong. The petals are pages of the assignment that God has written for us.

On Target

I felt the Lord saying...
"Take flight. You are on target with your assignments, but watch for distractions that will lead you from your goal. With my nectar of honey that you receive, feed the hearts around you with my love. The seeds are ready for planting. You are my disciple, so follow the Son."

But for you who revere my name, the sun of righteousness will rise with healing in its wings.
Malachi 4:2 (ESV)

Dear daughter,

As I was sitting with the Lord, He blessed me with this beautiful vision of a diamond. All the sparkling colours of the rainbow represent His promises. Pouring out from the glistening diamond was a single teardrop. Encased in this tear was the tree of life with many roots. Then I saw the Holy Spirit hovering.

My Prized Diamond

I felt the Lord saying...

"You are my prized diamond, shining brightly with my love's colourful promises. Every shade of colour glistens like a tear drop. I have seen your tears that you have shed as a young girl, because you did not have your earthly father's love. But I have held you in my arms with unconditional love and I was always singing your song over you. From your tears, your faith was birthed, and my tree of life was established and has taken root in your life. The roots have grounded you, holding you tightly to keep you safe and loved. I was always there to guide you through your fragile years. The Holy Spirit is there, enveloping you and giving you courage. You have a mighty gift from the heavenlies. It is shining bright like the precious diamond that you are."

SINCE YOU ARE PRECIOUS AND HONORED IN MY SIGHT, AND BECAUSE I LOVE YOU, I WILL GIVE PEOPLE IN EXCHANGE FOR YOU, NATIONS IN EXCHANGE FOR YOUR LIFE.
ISAIAH 43:4 (NIV)

Dear Daughter,

God showed me a beautiful vision of an open heaven through an open door. Flowing from this open door were rivers of colours. The colours poured out and became one, united, and then poured through the handle of an ancient key. The key was about to be inserted into a lock. This lock would then open a destiny. Every part of the flowing river had been an integral part of combining tools of knowledge to create the courage to turn the key and unlock God's plans.

The journey for the key to unlock

The orange represents the courage to turn the lock. White represents the purity to step into what God has planned. Purple represents accepting the royalty of your inheritance. Yellow represents bringing fire to the calling. Red represents the river of God's love and Jesus' sacrifice. Blue represents being filled with the word of God to bless others with your faith of healing. Green represents the new beginnings that will happen so you can leave the past behind. Gold represents being filled with God's glory and majesty.

"…I have heard your prayer and seen your tears; I will heal you…" 2 Kings 20:5 (NIV)

You have turned for me my mourning into dancing; you have loosed my sackcloth and clothed me with gladness, that my glory may sing your praise and not be silent. O Lord my God, I will give thanks to you forever! Psalm 30:11-12 (ESV)

Dear Daughter

I was in prayer with the Lord asking Him what was on His heart for me. Feeling alone and vulnerable, He showed me an image of myself kneeling and crying out to Him, and there appeared above me a giant feathered wing. Rain was falling down and saturating my being.

Protection

I felt the Lord saying... "I am always covering you with my protection and my love. I am pouring out my living water to saturate your fragile being. Never doubt me. I see every nuance of pain and every tear that you shed. Draw on my strength and take refuge in me. I hold you close and will never forsake you."

He shall cover you with His feathers and under His wings you shall take refuge
Psalm 91:4 NIV

Dear daughter,

As I sat with the Lord, pouring out my heart's past hurts, He told me to cast off my pain and renew my strength by resetting my mindset and speaking out His truth. As I praise God, He cloaks me in a silk robe of courage and an extra shoulder robe to shrug off bitterness. The robe flows effortlessly like pure silk, representing honour and glory. My robe then turns into the strong buttress roots of a tree with the abundant growth of a new direction. I am strong and centred in the grounding of God's word.

Growth

I felt the Lord saying...

"Turn your shoulder on past hurts and past criticisms. You are my precious daughter and I am clothing you with my righteousness. My yoke is easy, and I am giving you this new mantle to carry out my plans. It flows comfortably like silk. It won't slip off and fall. It is part of you just as I am in you. The plaited hair is a reminder of the little girl of the past. She has won the victory because she is matured in her faith and knows she is the daughter of the Most High."

For every word Yahweh speaks is sure and reliable. His truth is tested, found to be flawless, and ever faithful. It's as pure as silver refined seven times in a crucible of clay. Lord, you will keep us safe, out of the reach of the wicked.
Psalm 12:6-7 TPT

Dear daughter,

The Lord put it on my heart to draw a beautiful rose that is fully grown in all its glory. Then I felt to create the illusion of precious gems encased in the centre of the flower. This is the beauty inside of us —our gifts and our love for others. As it emerges, we shine brightly for Jesus. Then a few weeks later the Lord showed me this vision of a budding rosebud amongst the hurting and the needy. I felt these two pictures were related. With the rosebud painting I blurred the dead roses; they were once lifeless. But they are now being saturated by the love of the one who stands brightly—the rosebud. The gems from the first flower are birthed in the rosebud and they continue to bless the fully grown rose. The rosebud has been blessed and she shares her gifts.

We always have God's blessings, freely share these gifts with others and see them come alive with the love of the Father.

The Lord creates His beautiful masterpiece, beginning with a rosebud that then blossoms into the fully grown rose she was destined to be. As the rosebud grows, so does her inner beauty. The sparkling gems of her life are seen. They cannot contain the brilliance of the light so they shine for Jesus. Shine brightly. Don't hide your gifts under a bush. Your gifts are your gems.

I am truly His Rose

I felt the Lord saying...
"You are a crisp and newly formed rose bud, sprouting for all those around to see. You are entwined with the holy journey God has you on. Those around you are withered, lifeless, and thirsty for a touch of heaven. You bring a fresh anointing to their tired souls to shine brightly with the hope of Jesus."

I will stay close to you,

instructing and guiding you
along the pathway for your life.
I will advise you along the way
and lead you forth with my eyes
as your guide.

Ps. 32:8-9 TPT

Dear daughter

As I was praying and drawing with God one morning, He gave me a vision of a giant paintbrush painting the world.
He started to encourage me to spread my gift of prophetic art around the world.

Your gifts are priceless and need to be shared with the world. Enter into His presence and receive the love of the Lord to go forward and paint the world with the embellishing hope of Jesus Christ. The Lord is not finished with your life and wants to flood you with grace gifts to share His love with so many. Paint, write, sing, speak, serve, mend, love and give! The Lord will show you how this is done.
HE is with YOU.

I will stay close to you, instructing and guiding you along the pathway for your life. I will advise you along the way and lead you forth with my eyes as your guide
Psalm 32: 8-9 TPT

Come with me to paint the earth

The Trinity is complete in this vision:

The giant paintbrush is held by the Father, directing the tidal wave of peace and goodness. As you share your gifts with the world, the outcome is in God's hands.

The cross is at the centre, with the blood of Jesus dominating the wave of love. The power and surge from these acts of obedience result in a powerful tsunami that whitewashes the world with God's presence. It also cleanses the world, bringing people deeper into God's presence to be fully aligned with Him.

There is a clarity on earth, an explosion of revelation. The Holy Spirit envelopes the earth while Jesus tenderly holds the earth because He came to sacrifice His life for us. Share your gifts with the world and watch how God multiplies the fruit of your

"yes."

ALL DOWN

Dear daughter,

The Lord was showing me in this vision to lay it all down. I saw a beautiful, strong wooden mahogany table with very strong legs supporting the top of the table. The Bible was sitting open in the centre of the table. However, there was too much rubbish cluttering up the table. God asked me, "What are your idols?" The idols need to be put in the trash bin and the table needs to be cleared, so that the beauty of the word of the Lord can be seen, read and experienced.

As the table is cleared, new life and new growth commenced, entwining around the foundation of the legs of the table. There is a birthing of holy flowers, which flourish and then grow upward to the tabletop. There is an embracing of clarity and a cleansing of the slate. Through this I saw a crystal clear river with refreshing living water coming over and enveloping the space. The river turned into mountains in the background, and I saw this as the journey and the assignments that God has for all His children. The Lord is inviting you to get rid of your idols, putting them in the trash, so there would be clarity to hear your heavenly Father's voice.

Lay it all down

I felt the Lord saying…
"Acts of obedience bring life. Lay it all out on the table-your cares, your worries, addictions, and idols. Seek His word, and let His breath of life fill you, rather than worldly pleasures and idols. Empty it out before the Lord, put it in the trash and be led to a river of cleansing."

No temptation has overtaken you except what is common to mankind. And God is faithful; he will not let you be tempted beyond what you can bear. But when you are tempted, he will also provide a way out so that you can endure it. Therefore, my dear friends, flee from idolatry.
1 Cor. 10:13-14 NIV

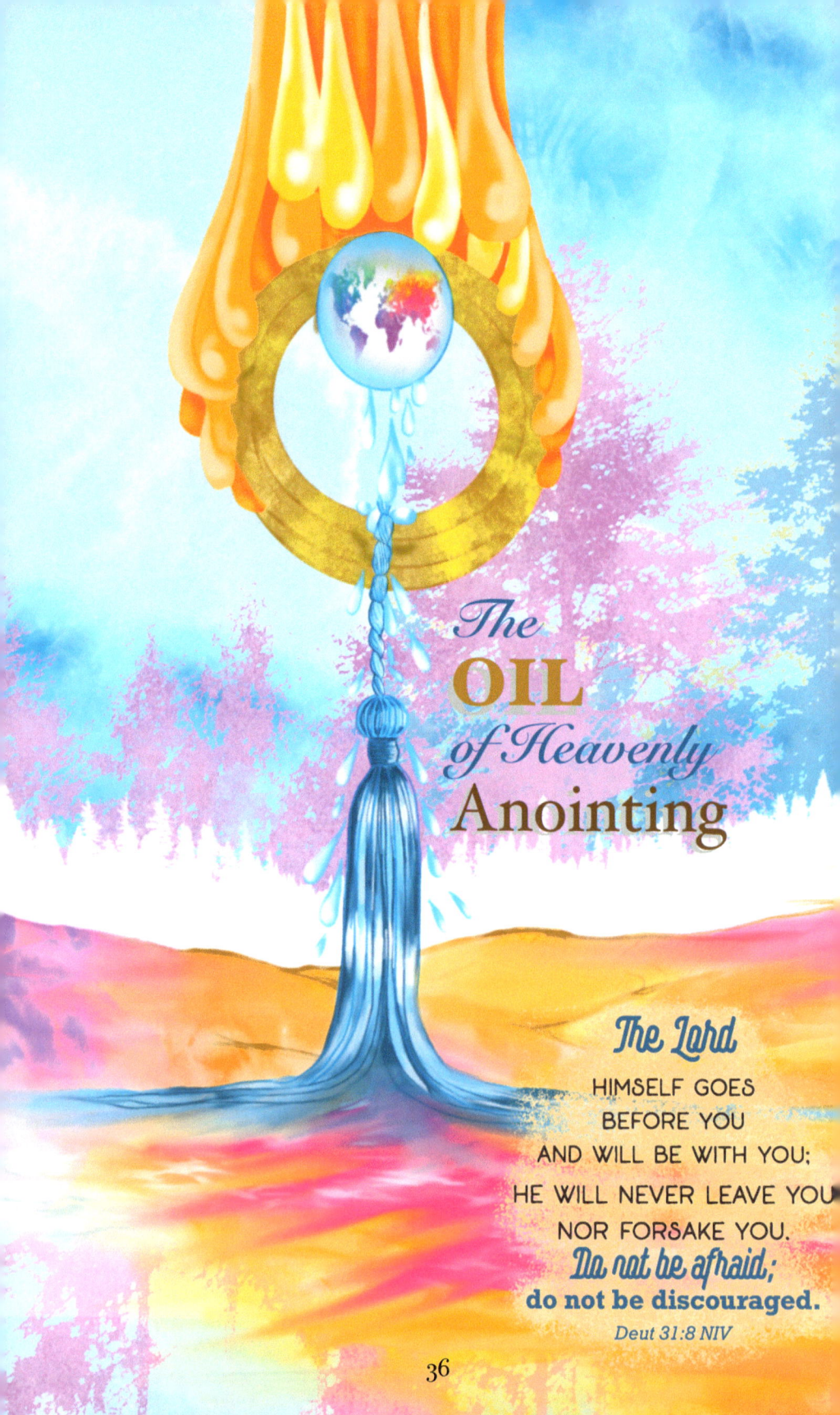

Dear daughter

The oil of heavenly anointing and fragrance is pouring down from the heavens, preparing the way for all that is to be done. This is the preparation for His mighty plans to be birthed. The anointing oil will touch hearts, smoothing out any darkness and negative past thoughts. The living water is running down, cleansing the pure white canvas, and making it ready to unleash His masterpiece. The golden handle will open the door to His love, glistening with His tears, shed for His children. The circular handle is the completeness that encapsulates His love for the one. The blue tassel hangs elegantly with the statement of all His sacrifices made for our healings. The tassel turns into rivers of His love and joy. Pull the handle and open the door into all that God has for you. He has gone before you.

Dear daughter,

God showed me a beautiful and powerful vision. There was a solid brick wall, and on each brick there was a label of past sins. God reminded me that the Spirit of life flowing through the anointing of Jesus has liberated us from the law of sin. Jesus' hand is holding a nail, representing his crucifixion. With His blood, He paid the price for our sins. These nails hammered away the accusing voice of condemnation. Let new life transform your mindset.

condemnation

I felt the Lord saying...
"Stop harbouring the guilt of past sins. Don't store them up by building a brick wall that is a monument to your sin. Through the sacrifice of our Saviour, He has abolished the curse of sin. He is living His life in us. He has given us the freedom to live, not according to our flesh, but according to the power of the Holy Spirit."

Yes, God raised Jesus to life! And since God's Spirit of Resurrection lives in you, he will also raise your dying body to life by the same Spirit that breathes life into you! So then, beloved ones, the flesh has no claims on us at all, and we have no further obligation to live in obedience to it. For when you live controlled by the flesh, you are about to die. But if the life of the Spirit puts to death the corrupt ways of the flesh, we then taste his abundant life.
Romans 8:11-13 TPT

Dear daughter

As I was reflecting with the Lord, He showed me a complete circle and I knew this was a representation of God. It then became a glistening pearl, tenderly held by His hands. The pearl became a magnolia flower that was emerging into the final beauty of His masterpiece. I proceeded to paint this vision with watercolour, using delicate pinks to represent the layers being healed. This is how God sees us—in layers—and He fine tunes and carefully peels back the layers to showcase our beauty. The yellow centre is the final glory that shines from our inner self after all of our layers are released. The leaves are His hands reverently holding His daughter for all the chapters of her life.

Chapters of our life

I felt the Lord saying…
"Let go and let God work on healing your worldly layers so that you can release to those around you the beauty of who you truly are….
A daughter of the King."

The Lord your God will circumcise your hearts and the hearts of your descendants, so that you may love him with all your heart and with all your soul, and live.
Deut. 30:6 NIV

The eternal God is your refuge, and underneath are the everlasting arms.
Deut. 33:27 NIV

His Beloved

He has called us and made us his very own beloved children.
1 John 3:1. TPT

Dear daughter,

I had a vision of a small ugly duckling. Then my heavenly Father showed me how He sees me. I had grown into this glorious, beautiful swan~a beloved daughter of the Most High.

His Beloved

If only we could see ourselves how God see us. In His sight we are beautiful, graceful, gifted and a perfectly loved child of God. We are powerful because we have Christ inside of us.
We can do anything with His help and guidance.

1 John 3:1. TPT
Look with wonder at the depth of the Father's marvellous love that He has lavished on us! He has called us and made us His very own *beloved children.*

Luke 1:37 ESV
For nothing will be impossible with God.

Strength

For I can do everything through Christ, who gives me strength

Phil. 4:13 NLT

Dear daughter

As I felt the nudging of Jesus to start drawing, I pencilled a sketch of a leaf, and as I began to draw the veins of the leaf, I felt the Father's heart. I realised I was drawing myself; this is how the Father sees us. There is a fragility and delicateness in the leaf, but the Father is the backbone of its strength. We cannot do anything without Him. There is a strength about this leaf. It is standing tall and erect, challenging what's ahead and ready for the battle. The leaf has a colourful story of new growth.
There is a new page for every step.

Strength

I felt the Lord saying...
"You are my delicate leaf, and I am your backbone of strength. Holding you together are the veins—an integral part of your giftings for the paths that I have you on. I am equipping you for every step of your assignment and nothing has been in vain. You are becoming stronger by feeding off the sun that shines brightly throughout your journey toward your home. The background is arranged in colourful oranges, representing courage and glistening in His brilliance."
Know that He has your every step.

It is God who arms me with strength and keeps my way secure. He makes my feet like the feet of a deer; he causes me to stand on the heights. He trains my hands for battle; my arms can bend a bow of bronze. You make your saving help my shield; your help has made me great.
2 Sam 22:33 NIV

Dear daughter,

I was praying with the Lord one morning and I felt anxiety and sadness. The Lord straight away showed me a beautiful vision of open flowers. These flowers greet the day with gay abandon, opening their faces up to the sun.

Anxiety and gloom is nowhere to be seen-only a trusting openness to receive the blessings of a new day. The colour was glorious, bringing the joy of God's beautiful creations.

Something so simple can bring a smile to your face as you reflect on the goodness and love of our heavenly Father.

How can we not smile when we feel His overwhelming presence and love? Rejoice!

Rise and Shine

Rise up and shine, for your light has come. The shining-greatness of the Lord has risen upon you. For see, darkness will cover the earth. Much darkness will cover the people. But the Lord will rise upon you, and His shining-greatness will be seen upon you.
Isaiah 60:1-2 (NLV)

Dear daughter

I was in prayer for many broken women that I was called to minister to and God gave me a simple vision of a woman's foot taking a step of freedom. Her skirt was billowing around her feet as though a curtain was being torn. The chains were broken, and she was free to step out into the path the Lord had for her.

FREEDOM - CHAINS WILL BE BROKEN.

I felt the Lord saying...
"I have given you the key to unlock your chains.
Be bold and use that key to unshackle the chains binding you to hurt.
Step into forgiveness and let go of past hurts to receive all that I have for you. What is holding you back?
Break free and feel the freedom of being the beloved daughter of the King.
Wear your crown and use the authority you have through your identity in Christ."

NOW THE LORD IS THE SPIRIT,
AND WHERE THE SPIRIT OF
THE LORD IS, THERE IS
FREEDOM.
2 COR. 3:17 NIV

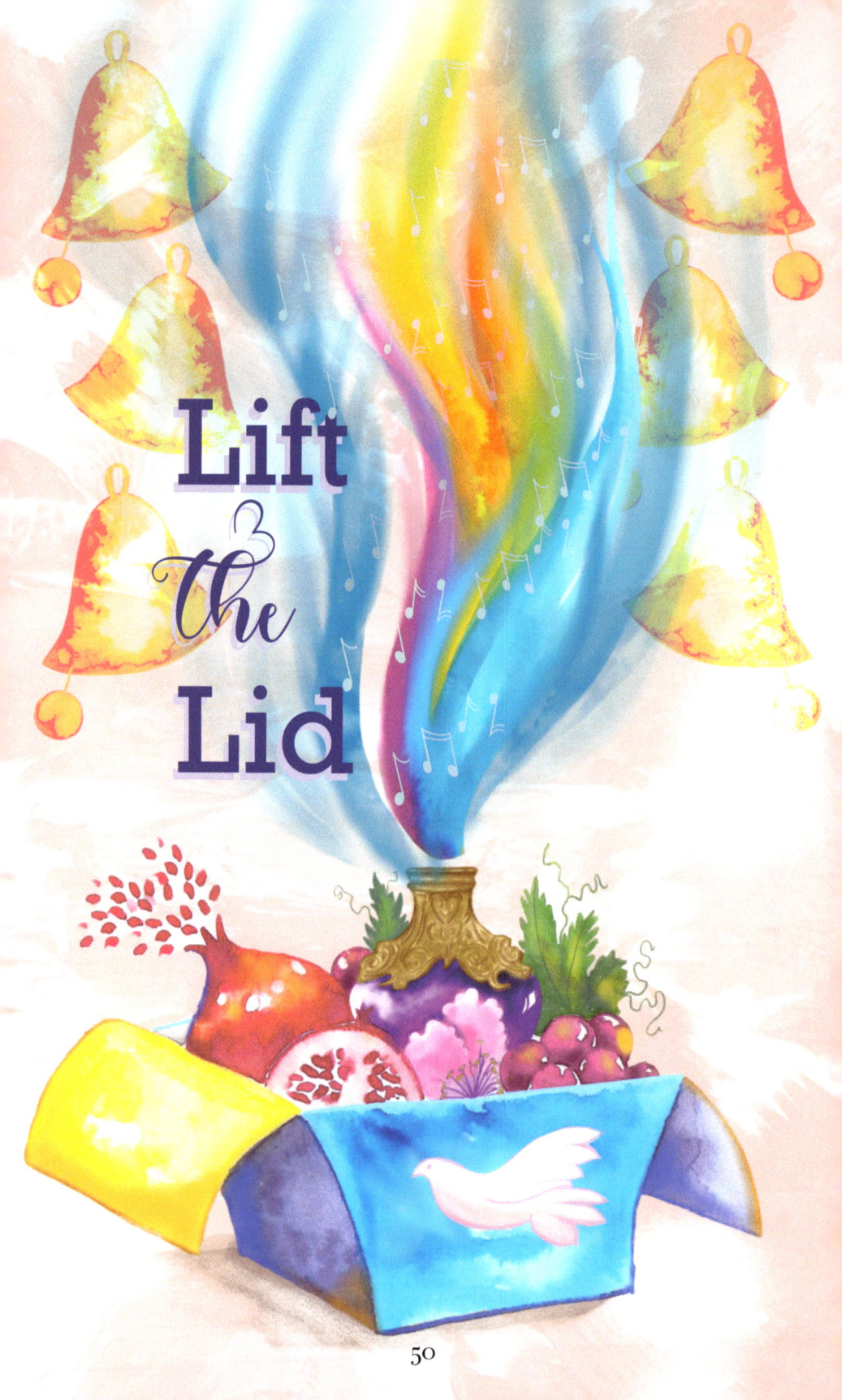

Dear daughter

I saw a vision of a box. The box was bending—it was pliable and ready to surrender. Out of the box came a triumphant sound of worship notes floating to the heavens, entwined with the perfume of our inner soul. I heard the sound of joyous bells. The box was filled with good fruit, including pomegranates. Pomegranates and bells pictures were adorned on the hem of priestly garments.

Lift the lid

•

I felt the Lord saying...
"The Lord said to open the box. Too many boxes have been closed. They have been sealed—closed to my word, closed to my heart, and hardened by life's hardships. God desires to lift off the lids of complacency that you are under and awaken you to your senses of hearing, seeing, and smelling His visions through the invitation of His hand leading you out of the darkness. As you lift up your praises, God's love pours down.

Open your box and let your praise and giftings be free to worship the King. Let your sweet smelling perfume arise to honour our King.

Wear your priestly garments to ring the bell so others will hear my voice. The pomegranates are your fruitfulness and the seeds you are planting. You are adorning the temple, creating a purity and a reverence to my word."

Your inward life is now sprouting, bringing forth fruit. What a beautiful paradise unfolds within you. When I'm near you, I smell aromas of the finest spice, for many clusters of my exquisite fruit now grow within your inner garden.
Song of Songs 4:13-14 TPT

Dear daughter,

After guiding some women through a healing and prophetic art workshop, I was in prayer about the ones who had been healed. God showed me this simple vision of a broken heart being stitched together. There were vines and scatterings of flowers. There was a pure white background with an intentional design of leaves.

Healing Hearts

I felt the Lord saying…
"I am always healing the brokenhearted. I may bring someone into your life for this very purpose. Know that I feel your pain and your brokenness and I see the tears you shed. I am renewing your heart. My tapestry needle is weaving to and fro, purposely stitching every torn part of your heart. The thread is purple, representing your royalty. You are my daughter. As the thread binds the broken pages of your life, there is a blossoming of new chapters. The vine is my surrounding love and protection, always birthing new hope and joy into your life. There is an abundance of pure golden glory miracles scattered throughout your victorious life."

Dear daughter

As I was praying one day and asking the Lord how He saw my calling, He gave me this beautiful vision. I saw a hand holding an oyster, and inside the oyster was a huge pearl. The pearl also looked like the earth, and there was oil dripping down and surrounding it. Oil is a powerful symbol in the Bible, representing divine blessings, protection, healing, and the presence of the Holy Spirit. There was also a life story of colours developing within the oyster.

The world is your oyster

I felt the Lord saying…
"I have you cradled in the palm of my hand. There is a strong protection covering you. You are nestled in my safe house, represented by the oyster shell. The pearl is sitting in and floating on top of my oil. It is buoyant. The oil represents the daily nourishment of my love but also the grounding, a daily growing, and a crushing for your refinement. There is more refinement and more major pressing to come that will produce this oil to fan your flame. Keep this fire burning and keep pressing in. Follow my lead and my promptings. This journey is not what you think. Trust me in the path I have you on. The oil is dripping onto the nations, representing the work that you are doing with me. I see the big picture from the beginning to the end. Trust your gift. It won't go unused."

For this reason I remind you to fan into flame the gift of God, which is in you through the laying on of my hands. For God did not give us a spirit of timidity, but a spirit of power, of love and of self-discipline.   2 Timothy 1:6-7 NIV

This book is lovingly published by
LIONHEART MINISTRY
www.lionheartministry.com

Thank You

I would love to sincerely thank the Lionheart Ministry team. Without their encouragement and generosity this book would not have been published. Thank you for believing in my ministry of prophetic art. Carrie tirelessly pushes women to fulfil their artistic, Godly destinies for the Kingdom. She has an anointed gift of words that birth the heavenly imagination to step into God's presence.

I would also like to thank the talented and gifted Lindsey Sullivan. Lindsey is such a unique gift to me and so many, a talented songwriter and musician, journalist and artist. Her help with the graphic design and editing was invaluable.

I thank my husband John Hudson, for his endless loving encouragement and support, and belief in my giftings.

Lynne Hudson

Lynne has been a professional artist for over forty years. Her work includes creating private painting commissions for clients. She has a special love for illustrating children's books, including Christian books and media. Lynne has been humbled to have held many successful art exhibitions with her works, including exhibitions in Australia and New York City.

Her journey has embraced a love and joy of prophetic art, from live painting with worship, to private commissions, to teaching courses on the magnitude of hearing from God through creativity. Lynne paints the promises of God in the prophetic positioning and power of the Lord, radiantly displaying artwork from on high.

Lynne resides on the Gold Coast, Queensland, Australia. Connect with Lynne at www.lynnehudson.com

If you would like to know Jesus, and have a relationship with him, say this simple prayer.

Dear Jesus,
I realise I need you. I believe you died for my sins and that you rose again. I ask you to come into my heart and be my Lord and saviour. I repent of my sins and I put you first in my life. Thank you for saving me.
In Jesus name, Amen

And I pray that he would unveil within you the
unlimited riches of his glory and favor until
supernatural strength floods your innermost being
with his divine might and explosive power. Then, by
constantly using your faith, the life of Christ will be
released deep inside you, and the resting place of
his love will become the very source and root of your
life. Then you will be empowered to discover what
every holy one experiences—the great magnitude
of the astonishing love of Christ in all its dimensions.
How deeply intimate and far-reaching is his love! How
enduring and inclusive it is!
Endless love beyond measure that transcends
our understanding—this extravagant love pours into
you until you are filled to overflowing with
the fullness of God!

Ephesians 3:16-19 (TPT)